W9-BLU-137

Welcome to **Spain**

By Mary Berendes

The
**Child's
World**

Published by The Child's World®
1980 Lookout Drive
Mankato, MN 56003-1705
800-599-READ
www.childsworld.com

Content Adviser: Professor Gichana C. Manyara, Department of Geography,
Radford University, Radford, VA
Design and Production: The Creative Spark, San Juan, Capistrano, CA
Editorial: Emily J. Dolbear, Brookline, MA
Photo Research: Deborah Goodsite, Califon, NJ

Cover and title page photo: Steve Vidler/SuperStock
Interior photos: Alamy: 12 (Chad Ehlers), 14 (Jon Arnold Images), 17 (Edward Parker), 20
(Peter Jordan), 21 (Richard Wareham Fotografie), 23 (Jeff Greenberg); Art Resource: 11
(Erich Lessing); Corbis: 13 (Dany Virgili/Spanish Royal House/epa); Getty Images: 7 (Peter
Wilson/Dorling Kindersley); The Image Works: 6 (Larry Mangino), 10 (Roger-Viollet), 18 (Bob
Daemmrich), 24 (Larry Mangino); iStockphoto.com: 9 (Joop Snijder), 16 (Duncan Walker), 22
(Roberto Adrian), 28 (Gioadventures), 29 (Manuel Velasco), 31 (Daniel Silva); Jupiterimages:
3 middle, 8 (Michael Leach/Oxford Scientific), 3 bottom, 25 (Sime s.a.s./eStock Photo); Lonely
Planet Images: 19 (Juliet Coombe), 3 top, 30 (Damien Simonis); NASA Earth Observatory:
4 (Reto Stockli); Panos Pictures: 15 (Alfredo Caliz); SuperStock: 27 (age fotostock).
Map: XNR Productions: 5

Library of Congress Cataloging-in-Publication Data
Berendes, Mary.
  Welcome to Spain / by Mary Berendes.
      p. cm. — (Welcome to the world)
  Includes index.
  ISBN 978-1-59296-979-1 (library bound : alk. paper)
  1. Spain—Juvenile literature. [1. Spain.] I. Title. II. Series.

DP17.B48 2008
946—dc22

                                                    2007038280

Contents

Where Is Spain?

If you could fly high above Earth, what would you see? If you looked closely, you would notice huge land areas with water all around them. These land areas are called **continents.** Some continents are made up of many different countries.

Spain is a country on the continent of Europe.

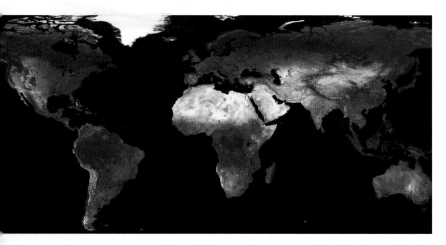

This picture gives us a flat look at Earth. Spain is inside the red circle.

4

The Land

Spain has many types of land. There are sandy beaches. There are flat, often treeless lands called **plains.** There are even high, rocky cliffs. Much of Spain is a huge, dry area called the Meseta (may-SAY-tuh). The Meseta is really a

The Spanish area known as the Meseta

plateau. A plateau is a flat area of land that is higher than the land around it.

Spain also has beautiful mountains. The Pyrenees (PEER-uh-neez) mountain range lies in the north of Spain. The steep slopes are covered with green forests. They also contain many clear waterfalls. Farther south, on the Canary Islands, is Spain's highest mountain. Pico de Teide (PEE-koh day tee-YAY-day) reaches 12,198 feet (3,718 meters) high.

A village church near the Pyrenees

7

Plants and Animals

White storks nest in Spain.

Much of Spain is very warm and dry. Tall trees and green plants do not grow in those areas. Instead, the land is covered with small bushes and grasses. But in the mountains, green forests of pine and evergreen trees grow.

Spain is home to many kinds of animals. In the mountains, bears, wolves, foxes, and lynx prowl. In Spain's hotter areas, snakes, rabbits, and lizards can be found. Many types of birds live in Spain, too. In fact, white storks often build huge nests in the high towers of churches and other tall buildings!

Pine trees grow in a national park in Spain.

Long Ago

People have been living in Spain for more than 100,000 years. About 5,000 years ago, a group of people called the **Iberians** lived in Spain. Over time, many other groups came to the country, including the Celts (KELTS), the Greeks, the Romans, and the Moors. Some people were looking for new places to live. Others wanted to find gold or other riches.

Spain soon became a very powerful country. It had kings and queens

A stone carving of an Iberian woman

This painting shows explorer Christopher Columbus climbing the stairs to meet with Spain's king and queen.

and a strong army. Spain also sent explorers, including Christopher Columbus, to travel the world. Spain controlled many other countries. Slowly, though, other people began to rule these countries. Spain had lost its power.

This statue shows people doing a special dance from the Catalonia region. The city of Barcelona is in the background.

Spain Today

Today, Spain is a growing country. Instead of trying to rule other countries, Spain is working to improve life for its own citizens. People in some regions of Spain want more independence. But most Spanish people are working together to make their country strong and proud.

Just as it did long ago, Spain has a king. But Spain's king does not have very much power. Instead, a prime minister leads the country. The prime minister and the rest of the government make laws to keep Spain safe.

Spain's King Juan Carlos I and Queen Sofía in 2007

The People

Most Spaniards are relatives of the first groups that lived in Spain. Others are **immigrants,** or newcomers from other places. Many immigrants are from other countries in Europe. Others are from Latin American countries such as Ecuador

Spanish girls wear costumes for a fair in Jerez de la Frontera.

and Colombia. They also come from African countries such as Morocco.

Spanish people are happy and fun-loving. In Spain, relaxing and having a good time are very important. But working hard and studying are important, too.

This local soccer team includes some immigrants from Ecuador.

Did you know?

Spanish people love to visit with friends and family. In fact, most people enjoy a peaceful stroll called a *paseo* (pah-SAY-oh) before their evening meal. During the paseo, friends share stories about their day.

A city street in Madrid

City Life and Country Life

A Spanish farmer uses a donkey to carry cork from the forest.

Most of Spain's people live in cities, where almost everyone lives in apartments. There are many interesting things to do in the cities. People visit museums, shop, eat at restaurants, and go to concerts and movies. Life is simpler in Spain's countryside.

Most of Spain's country people are farmers who live in small towns or villages. Houses are often made from clay and stones, just as they were long ago. There is less electricity and modern equipment in the Spanish countryside. Even so, the country people enjoy what they do.

Schools and Language

Spanish children begin school when they are about six years old. They study reading, writing, and math. They also learn about history and science. Most students in Spain go to school until they are 16 years old.

A sign in Catalan, Spanish, and English

Spain's official language is Spanish. In different areas of Spain, certain words are pronounced differently. In three northern areas of Spain, other languages are used, too. People there speak Catalan, Basque (BASK), or Galician (ga-LISH-un). These beautiful languages are very old.

18

Schoolchildren gather in Madrid's central square, called the *Puerta del Sol* or "Gate of the Sun."

A worker uses a metal grinding tool at a Barcelona truck plant.

Work

Spaniards have many different jobs. Some people work in factories. They help to make such things as cars, cement, ships, shoes, and clothes. Other Spanish people have jobs in restaurants, shops, and offices.

Some people in Spain work as farmers. They grow such things as oranges, sugar beets, and wine grapes. Spain is one of the world's largest olive producers. There are lots of different kinds of work to do in Spain!

HORARIO DE LUNES A VIERNES BUSINESS HOURS FROM MONDAY TO FRIDAY		
Mañanas - Morning	09.30	13:30
Tardes - Afternoon	16:30	20:00
Sábados - Saturday	10.00	13.00

Did you know?

During the hot midday hours, Spaniards often take rests called *siestas* (see-YES-tahs). During the siesta, shops and businesses close (left). A few hours later, people return to work to finish the day. In many areas, the siesta is still a very important part of the day.

21

Food

Spanish people love seafood. Crabs, sardines, squid, and baby eels are all favorite foods in Spain. Many people also like to eat meat and fresh fruit and vegetables. One dish, called **paella** (pah-AY-yuh), mixes lots of things together. It is made with rice, shrimp, chicken, lobster, ham, and vegetables.

Spanish *paella*

Wine is a very popular drink in Spain. Spanish people also like soft drinks. One of the most popular things to drink in Spain is a thick hot chocolate. It is often served with a treat called **churros** (CHOO-rros). Churros are strips of fried dough sprinkled with sugar.

A fruit and vegetable market in Madrid

A soccer league plays on the beach in northern Spain.

Pastimes

Spaniards love to spend time outside. They like to take walks and go on picnics. The Spanish people love sports, too—especially soccer. In fact, many big cities have soccer stadiums that seat more than 100,000 people!

One of the oldest sports in Spain is bullfighting. In a bullfight, a **matador** (MAT-uh-dor) stands in a ring with a large bull. He or she waves a brightly colored cape to anger the animal. The matador quickly moves out of the way when the bull charges. Matadors who are brave and strong during their bullfights can become very famous in Spain.

Did you **know?**

One famous dance in Spain is called the *flamenco* (above). During the dance, dancers stomp their feet and clap their hands loudly. They twirl and twist to the music of a guitar. The flamenco is hundreds of years old.

25

Holidays

Spaniards celebrate many holidays. One special holiday is called the *Fiesta de San Fermín* (fee-YES-tah day SAN fer-MEEN), or "the Festival of Saint Fermín." Thousands of people come to the city of Pamplona every year to celebrate this holiday. Every morning from July 7 to 14, bulls are released to run in the streets of the city. Some people even try to run with the bulls!

Spain is a country known for its sunny weather, rolling lands, and happy people. Maybe one day you will travel to Spain's beautiful mountains. Or perhaps you will watch a bullfight in an old Spanish town. Or maybe you will sample a huge dish of paella. Whatever you do, Spain is sure to keep you busy!

Some people run with the bulls during the Fiesta de San Fermín.

Area: 194,897 square miles (504,782 square kilometers)—about twice the size of Oregon

Population: More than 40 million people

Capital City: Madrid

Other Important Cities: Barcelona, Valencia, Seville, Saragossa, and Málaga

Money: The euro. On January 1, 2002, the euro became the only money used in daily business for countries that are members of the European Monetary Union.

National Languages: Spanish; Catalan, Galician, and Basque are official in their regions

National Holiday: National Day on October 12 (1492)

National Flag: Two stripes of red with a yellow stripe between them. The national coat of arms was added in 1981. It appears in the middle of Spain's flag.

Head of Government: The prime minister of Spain

Head of State: The king of Spain

Famous People:

Pedro Almodóvar: film director

Santiago Calatrava: architect

Camilo José Cela: winner of the Nobel Prize for Literature in 1989

Penélope Cruz: actor

Plácido Domingo: opera singer

Ferdinand V: king of Castile from 1474 to 1504 (later Ferdinand II of Aragon)

Julio Iglesias: singer

Isabella I: queen of Castile from 1474 to 1504

Severo Ochoa: cowinner of the Nobel Prize for Medicine in 1959

Pablo Picasso: artist

Juan Ponce de León: explorer

Arantxa Sánchez Vicario: tennis player

National Song: "The Royal March" or *"Marcha Real."* It became Spain's national song in 1942. The song has no official words.

Spanish Recipe*: Natilla

This recipe is for a dessert called *natilla* (nah-TEE-yah). It's a Spanish custard.

4 eggs
4 cups milk
¾ cup sugar
4 teaspoons cornstarch
Rind of 1 lemon
1 cinnamon stick
Ladyfingers (small spongecake cookies)

Beat eggs, milk, sugar, and cornstarch in a bowl until frothy. Add lemon rind and cinnamon stick. Pour mixture into a medium-sized saucepan. Cook over medium heat until slightly thickened. Arrange ladyfingers around deep glass bowl. Remove lemon rind and cinnamon stick. Pour custard over ladyfingers. Sprinkle with cinnamon and sugar. Cool and serve.

*Always ask an adult for permission and help when using the kitchen.

How Do You Say...

ENGLISH	SPANISH	HOW TO SAY IT
hello	hola	OH-lah
good-bye	adiós	ah-dee-OHSS
please	por favor	POR fah-VOR
thank you	gracias	GRAH-see-uss
one	uno	OO-noh
two	dos	DOHSS
three	tres	TRAYSS
Spain	España	eh-SPAHN-yuh

30

Glossary

churros (CHOO-rros) Churros are strips of fried dough sprinkled with sugar. They are a favorite Spanish treat.

continents (KON-tih-nents) Earth's huge land areas are called continents. Spain is a country on the continent of Europe.

Iberians (eye-BEER-ee-unz) The Iberians were a group of ancient people. They lived in what is now Spain about 5,000 years ago.

immigrants (IM-ih-grents) Immigrants are people who move from one country to live in another. Some immigrants move to Spain.

matador (MAT-uh-dor) A matador is another word for a bullfighter. Spain is famous for its matadors.

paella (pah-AY-yuh) Paella is made with rice, shrimp, chicken, lobster, ham, and vegetables. It is a popular Spanish dish.

plains (PLAYNZ) Plains are flat, often treeless lands. Spain has many plains.

plateau (pla-TOH) A plateau is a flat land area that is higher than the land around it. Much of Spain is a huge plateau called the Meseta.

Further Information

Read It

Busby, Barbara Sheen. *Foods of Spain*. Detroit, MI: KidHaven Press, 2007.

Corwin, Jeff. *Into Wild Spain*. San Diego: Blackbirch Press, 2004.

Crosbie, Duncan, and Tim Hutchinson (illustrator). *Find Out About Spain*. Hauppauge, NY: Barron's Educational Series, 2006.

Taus-Bolstad, Stacy. *Spain in Pictures*. Minneapolis: Lerner Publishing Group, 2004.

Look It Up

Visit our Web page for lots of links about Spain:
http://www.childsworld.com/links

Note to Parents, Teachers, and Librarians: We routinely verify our Web links to make sure they are safe, active sites—so encourage your readers to check them out!

Index